THINK LIKE GOD

UNDERSTANDING YOUR ORIGINAL MIND

BY

DENITRA BROWN

For further information please contact Denitra Brown via email at
consultant@lblbgroup.com.

Imprint of Kingdom Thinking Enterprises
Distributed by Ingram Spark
Printed in the United States of America

Think Like God
Understanding Your Original Mind

First Printing 2019

Copyright © 2019 by Denitra Brown
Cover Design by: Elvedina Durmišević
Contact Cover Designer at http://thebookcoverdesigner.com/designers/betibup33/
Licensed by: Denitra Brown

ISBN: 978-1-7338644-0-4

Library of Congress Control Number: 2019903452

All rights are reserved. Except for the use of brief quotations for a book review, no part of this publication may be reproduced, stored in a retrieval system or transmitted in any form or by any means, electronic, mechanical, photocopying, recording or otherwise, without the prior written permission of the copyright owner.

Scripture references from King James Version of the Bible, unless otherwise noted. Copyright © 1990 by Thomas Nelson, Inc. Used by permission all rights reserved.

Scripture quotations marked TPT are from The Passion Translation®. Copyright © 2017, 2018 by Passion & Fire Ministries, Inc. Used by permission. All rights reserved. ThePassionTranslation.com

Scripture quotations marked NLT are taken from the Holy Bible, New Living Translation, copyright © 1996. Used by permission of Tyndale House Publishers, Inc., Wheaton, Illinois 60189. All rights reserved.

DEDICATION

To my Abba which art in Heaven for
knowing me before the world was made.
To my big brother Jesus Christ who always
has my back and allows me to reflect Him.
To my dear comforter the Holy Spirit who continues to
lead me into my purpose and has partnered with me.
Thank you for being ONE and for writing this book.

To my husband Robert:
God gave you to me to show me
His love toward me. I would not be
where I am today without your love.
You have ministered healing to me
life in an unexplainable way
never to be forgotten.

To our children:
Adriane, Bracy, Mia, Asa, Aliza, Jaya,
Isaiah, Joi, and Marie and the silent one.
- You all have saved my life! I am grateful to be a part of you and
you a part of me.

FOREWORD

I have long contended that our greatest ministry and message, is the life and experiences we have lived to date and our willingness to share it with others.

I grew up in a time (the 1950's) when the family was generally still intact. In other words, for the most part, homes were mostly comprised of a traditional father, mother, and children setting. There was a simplicity to life in part because God was still the center and focus of our lives.

Everything began to change beginning in the 1960s. Liberalism began to take root in marriage, sex, religion, and the family. From my perspective, it was the beginning of a move towards humanism and our falling away from God.

The family began to disintegrate, and Satan systematically began to remove fathers and men from the home. Removing prayer out of the school, and in many respects, out of the church. Men began to believe a lie rather than the truth. The church and God became more and more subverted and to publicly declare what God expected out of man became more and more unacceptable.

Due to "this great falling away" people... especially millennials and generation Xers did not grow up in homes where the ways of Christ and the Bible were taught.

This generation is not impressed with our "gifts of the spirit," or our ability to quote copious amounts of scriptures. Many do not know who Jesus is.

Today, we live in an "experience generated society." In other words, our testimonies are significantly more acceptable to the unsaved. Especially when you are willing to share and tell "YOUR story"!

People who don't know God today, are more moved by our story of deliverance from addictions, and vices that had us bound!

This phenomenon opens up the door for us to tell of the glory and goodness of God and how He saved us when we could not 'save' ourselves. We don't need a pulpit to do this.

I am so impressed with Denitra Brown's honesty, transparency, and openness. She seeks to "open the eyes of our understanding" with a personal and practical approach to God's thoughts of us. She doesn't attempt to preach to or condemn us, but from her own life's experiences, lets us know God still has expectations of us.

You'll find her stories of personal failure, attempted suicide, and rejection palpable and heart rendering. Let the words of her mouth, and the meditations of her heart, speak peaceably and comfortably to those of you whose lives are unfulfilled. This book and its references on how to "Think Like God" might be the vehicle you've been looking for to give insight, clarity, and guidance on how to bring fulfillment to your life.

Bishop James Laverne Tyson

Bishop J Laverne and Linda Tyson Ministries conduct Pastor's school, a monthly pastor wives' class, and a Ministers Clinic for aspiring ministers. Bishop J.L. Tyson is the author of numerous books including *People Who Shaped the Pentecostal Assemblies of the World*, *The Early Pentecostal Revival*, and *Whatever Happened to Your Dream* just to name a few.

TABLE OF CONTENTS

FORWARD	5
PREFACE	9
INTRODUCTION	11
CHAPTER 1: IF YOU ONLY KNEW	15
CHAPTER 2: JUST DO WHAT I SAY	27
CHAPTER 3: SIN, IT'S NOT WHAT YOU THINK	43
CHAPTER 4: BELIEVE OR UNBELIEF…YOU DECIDE	53
CHAPTER 5: REPENT, YOU WILL BE GLAD YOU DID	65
CHAPTER 6: HOW IT WORKS	71
DEFINITIONS	83

PREFACE

Have you stayed away from the church because you felt as if the things, they say don't make sense? Have you struggled with growing up in church only to conclude that some of the things you heard across the pulpit were not precisely true? Have you had a passion, and drive to succeed but can't figure out how to get there? These questions and others have circled the back of the minds of God's children long enough! Don't you think it is time to get some answers?

Within the unfolding pages of this book, we will look at some truths that have been unexplored in the past. These are not new truths mind you. They just have not been unfolded to a fuller capacity. This group of seekers will be bold enough, strong enough, courageous enough, and willing to unpack and embrace the certainties that lie within these page borders.

Warning, what you find may ruffle some feathers. That is okay. You are a generation with ambitions and zeal. You can afford to ruffle feathers here and there. Your shortcuts are for accuracy and efficiency. This book will get right to the heart of some specific areas of Christian understanding and truth.

Be encouraged to live, love, learn, and embrace the truth. Live the life you were meant to live by adopting a new way of thinking. This way of thinking will bring you the real success you desire!

INTRODUCTION

Greetings dear reader! Welcome to a brand-new way of living! Welcome to an entirely new way of thinking! Welcome to a dynamic new arena of exploration! Within the unfolding of these pages, you will find a new outlook on some ancient truths. By analyzing several words that will unfold before you and allow you to embrace a new way of thinking and thus a new way of living.

Not just any new way but if you implement the things we review here, you will begin to think just like God! That's right! If you have never understood that you could reason like God, do not be afraid. Be open! Reflect on the content within and go back to the scriptures to see if what you find here is true. You are bright, creative, and willing. We desire that you are equipped to live a truly abundant life.

Finally, on behalf of the "Christian Church" at large, I want to extend my sincerest apology and ask Jews, Gentiles, and Believers around the world to forgive the body of Christ for a spirit of error we have loosed over God's people. Our ancestors misrepresented His will, word, and love in ways that have affected the entire globe.

Mostly we began in error and unfortunately, we did not stand firm and speak against things once the truth was known. That flaw brought hurt, shame, brokenness, and misunderstanding to those within and without the church.

On the behalf of my Christian ancestors, I ask you to please forgive us. I repent on behalf of the pastor you once knew that led you astray. On behalf of church leaders who told you one thing and did another, I ask your forgiveness. If you were hurt and did not grow due to misleading in teachings, please forgive us. I ask that you do not hold it against God, the local pastor, and any other believer. I pray that you release us from any form of payment that you feel you deserve. In that, Christ himself can give you full retribution that He obtained for you long ago.

Now you are free to learn God for yourself. You can search the scriptures and understand what God is saying to you. You are now responsible for your soul salvation. You are free to learn, explore, and abide in the living God. I commit to thinking differently and by doing so, ensure my actions are different. The Lord loves you, and so do I.

Chapter 1

IF YOU ONLY KNEW

Since I was a child church was a part of my daily life. Growing up church services were offered at least four days per week and there was a myriad of auxiliary functions to choose from. I attended Sunday morning service, Sunday evening worship service, bible study, prayer meeting, usher board meeting, and choir rehearsal. It was also a given that as a youth one would serve as a junior usher, attend Christian elementary school, and/or participate in the children's choir. For as long as I could remember I have always loved God. Since the age of six I recall having conversations with God. By the age of twelve I found out that God had to be invited into the heart of man, and at first this seemed a little foreign to me because I was of the mindset that God was already with me. In fact, I had been talking to Him for years. I learned there was a difference, I began to understand that once I invited Him in, He dwelled within me. I was excited! God and I became best friends instantaneously and Jesus became my blood brother forever. The relationship that was formed allowed me to experience salvation and lead me on a path of wholeness.

Typically building longstanding relationships with people requires that you spend time, interacting with them on a personal level in order to really know them. The strange thing is relationship building is a lifelong process. No matter how long you know someone they can show you another side of themselves that you have never seen before. Even God can show you another side of Himself because he is so vast. My desire for you is to see and experience God from another vantage point and a new perspective. It is not because that side was not there or because it is new. On the contrary, it is because this is a new level of your relationship with Him. Your friendship is growing, there is an exchange between you and Him. So, rejoice and receive all that He is in you.

The Word of God tells us that God is not apart from his Word. Jesus is in the Father and the Father is in Him and we are in Christ thus we are in God as referenced in John 17:22-23 (Nelson, 1990). I love the thought of being the nucleus of God and He as the nucleus of me. He is such an amazing Father and force that we continue to grow in knowing Him and in coming to know who He is in our lives. This book will expound on the true meaning of five words that are found in the Holy Bible. Understanding the contextual meaning of these words changed my life and the way I perceived God and our relationship. I truly believe that sharing the insight I acquired from God's revelation will allow anyone who reads this to see and experience our Heavenly Father from a new perspective.

Warning! Some of the things I will share may contradict what you have always known or thought to be true. May I encourage you, do not bluntly reject it. Instead, become like the Berean Jews that Luke wrote about in Acts 17:10-11. Search the scriptures and study to see if what I share is factual. Ask God to allow you to earnestly receive His word and make it applicable and personal for you. You are made in His image after His likeness and you receive truth and you will not accept a lie. The words we will explore are as follows: knew, commandment, sin, unbelief, and repent.

In the *New King James Bible*, Jeremiah 1:5 says, "Before I formed thee in the belly, I *knew* thee; and before thou camest forth out of the womb I sanctified thee, and I ordained thee a prophet unto the nations." God is describing to Jeremiah and to us how He saw him before the foundations of the world. Before there were trees, rocks, dirt, and yes even people, God knew each and every one of us. What I love most about this word *knew* or "to know" is that, it not only describes how God knew us but how we knew Him in return. Let us dig in a little further.

The Strong's Exhaustive Concordance (SEC) describes *KNEW*/H3045 in Hebrew as Yadà. It is used in a variety of ways. In Jeremiah 1:5 *knew* is described as to ascertain by seeing, to observe, to care, to recognize, acknowledge, acquaintance, advise, answer, comprehend, cunning, diligent, discern, discover, endued with, familiar friend, perceive, prognosticate, regard, have respect, to teach and to understand, to name a few.

This *"knew"* describes Gods interaction with us before we were ever conceived. The author is telling us that God knew us by seeing us, He observed and cared for us. He recognized, acknowledged, and was acquainted with us as a familiar friend. He advised, answered, and comprehended us. He was cunning in His thoughts and development of us. He was diligent, discerning, and endued us with His Spirit. He discovered, perceived, regarded, and respected us. He taught, understood, and prophesied over us.

Can you see it now? As a thought in the endless time of God's perception He was thinking of you. His thoughts and promises are yes and let it be toward you, 2 Corinthians 1:20 (Passion, 2017). This is His prophetic over you. He saw you before you were born, and every day of your life was recorded in His book. He was and still is thinking of you with good thoughts as many as the grains of sand on the sea shore, and it has always been that way, Psalm 139:16-18 (Passion, 2017). These thoughts did not just happen because you were born but you were born because these were His thoughts toward you. He has a destiny and purpose for your life.

One of my favorite parts about His open care, concern, and love for you is that this word "knew" also reflects how you saw God before you were conceived. You had a relationship with God before you were thought of by your parents. As a matter of fact, this interaction with the Father was taking place before there was ever the first man and woman on the earth.

Not only did God see, observe, and care for you but you also saw, observed, and cared for God. You recognized, acknowledged, and were acquainted with Him as a familiar friend. You put your ideas on the table, answered, and comprehended Him. You were cunning in your ability to think and conversed about the development process of the kingdom*.

---

*In this book when referring to "kingdom" the reference is in the respect that a kingdom is a real place that has a live government and citizens. Please refer to the teachings of Dr. Myles Monroe for more insight into "the kingdom."

You were diligent, discerning, and endued by His Spirit. You discovered, perceived, regarded, and respected Him. You communicated, understood, and prophesied over Him.

You see, "Whosoever shall confess that Jesus is the Son of God, God dwelleth in him, and he in God. And we have known and believed the love that God hath to us. God is love; and he that dwelleth in love dwelleth in God, and God in him. Herein is our love made perfect, that we may have boldness in the day of judgement: because as He is so are, we in this world" (King James Version 1 John 4.15-17 capitalization added). That has always been the case. As He is, so are we in this world right now! We are made in His image after His likeness and are in the similitude of the one who made us. He empowered us with everything that pertains to life and godliness, 2 Peter 1:3 (Nelson, 1990) and we are seated in heavenly places with Christ Jesus, Eph. 2:6. You see He has always been with us, but the most fascinating thing is that we have always been with Him.

As we recognize our own position at the bountiful table and our original design; it is evident that we are gods, kings, lords, and heirs. His holy representatives in the earth to display to the world what it is like in heaven and what glorious benefits are offered to those who are engrafted into his marvelous kingdom. We are loved and admired by the creator of the universe. He has accepted us and given us a position at the table of heaven in His kingdom.

Once we receive Christ into our hearts, and we display love and faithfulness, we find favor with God and man, Prov. 3:3-4 (Passion, 2017). The fifteenth chapter of John conveys to us that we are positioned automatically in Him when we receive Him. We are encouraged to stay connected. We remain connected as we realize that God *knew* us and that we *knew* (and know) Him. There is an exchange between us and our creator. We have His DNA and He, our DNA. We are made in His image after His likeness and He breathed into us His breath of life. We are His holy people, a chosen nation, a royal priesthood because we have been engrafted and unified through His son, Jesus Christ.

Our relationship is an exchange between two individuals. We talk to Him and He speaks to us. We identify in Him and He in us, having the same open access as we did before we were "formed in the belly." Once we receive Christ, we are in Him and He is in us. We communicate with Him and He communicates with us. We perceive, respect, comprehend, and regard Him as He perceives, respects, and comprehends us. He now prophesy's over us and we prophesy over Him. When He releases prophetically over us, we know, understand, and have an insight to our future or the future around us. When we prophesy to Him, we release His will in the earth and declare to Him that His kingdom will come, and His will be done in earth just as it is in heaven, Matt. 6:10 (Nelson, 1990).

You may have never considered that you prophesy; especially to God. However, to prophesy or to prognosticate simply means to speak an inspired message. Many people prophesy without realizing it. When you encourage, esteem, and bless others with your words you are prophesying. Our prophetic words are always right when we declare what He says. We can never prophesy wrongly to our God when we say what He has given us to decree and verbally state according to his commandments.

Do you understand that your very destiny was discovered and discussed by you and the Father before the beginning? Your purpose in earth was settled and finalized before you ever got here. You have a particular seed inside of you. This seed that replicates your Father in heaven and His vision, purpose, and plan for your life. This seed reproduces itself in the image of God after His likeness and character within you. Nestled deep within yourself are the blueprints you and God conferred before the world formed. The plans design is to metamorphose and congeal according to the paths that you choose and in some cases that are chosen for you.

If you had two loving parents that cared, nurtured, and reared you up in the admonition of the Lord, they set you on a path of rightness or righteousness. That specific rearing up led you on a road that branched off into many different veins. The older you got, the more you had the opportunities to choose which threads you would follow. If you came from what we call a dysfunctional and broken home like I did where you felt you had to take care of yourself to survive or where you were mistreated as a child instead of nurtured; then you too were reared up and led on a path that branched off into many different veins. Depending on your personality, how you thought about yourself, and how you thought about your life determined which avenue you would choose.

At the age of six I had my first memory of being sexually abused by a family member. One day at school, I remember following a school official to an office where a lady began to ask me very personal questions about what was happening in my home. I answered her honestly. When I left the office, I was taken down the hallway where I passed my older brother going into the same office. Later that day I realized that my life was about to take a significant change. I was not to go home; instead a caseworker for the state drove me to what they called the Children's Guardian Home and I awaited to know what was next.

      The Guardian Home was a state-run facility which temporarily housed orphaned, dependent, abused and battered children from infants to eighteen until placement could be found with a family member or a foster home. This facility was a temporary stop on my new path, one that I did not choose. I was too young to regulate the destination but even that situation was written on my blueprint before the foundations of the world began and it would eventually work together for my good.

      No matter what vein you choose, or which one presents itself to you, your blueprint was designed to work all things "together for good to them that love God, to them who are the called according to His purpose" (Romans 8:28). You see, when you and the Father examined His plans and purpose for your life the conversation was with every scenario in mind that could happen to you based on who your ancestors were, what era you were born in, what purpose He assigned for you to fulfill, and even according to your personality. God uses all of these things concerning you and solidifies His goal for you through them.

The paths and veins you take in life determine where you will end. When you are a youth, you generally have no say over many things such as where you will live, who your parents are, where you will go to school, and even what you will eat from day to day. However, as you mature and become an adult, you now have authority, voice, and vision over your life. Your life has the opportunity to take many different paths and veins.

In the United States, you have the freedom to choose who you will marry. You can decide to marry a wonderful spouse who loves and nurtures you, or you can resolve to marry a spouse who is abusive and selfish. Where you have a free will to choose you are responsible for your actions and have the authority to dictate the outcomes. God knows you, and you know Him. As you are walking along the path, ask God to lead you only down the paths of righteousness. These are the paths most conducive for you. These paths are for His namesake and bring Him glory. Agree with Him concerning every way and all will be well.

Do not misunderstand, even as He leads you only down the paths of righteousness you will experience some hardships, challenges, and sufferings. This journey is okay and as part of the plan, will lead you into your greatest success. You see He will be with you throughout the entire process and will ensure you come out on top because He has chosen you and predestined your paths. He knows what you need to maneuver this plan. He knows you!

Knowing God includes you recognizing that at one point you already knew Him; you were already on that path of understanding. It is similar to when you reunite with an old friend whom you have not seen in years. You remember what you and He use to do and how you use to be with each other. After many years you change and so do, they but the reunion brings back fond memories where hope and excitement spring up within you to pick up from where you left off, and you now continue your long-term friendship.

My best friend from high school is Neesha. The reason she is my best friend is that when I was about fourteen years old, I prayed and asked God to send me a friend that was a Christian. Soon after that prayer a young lady came into my life and befriended me. I went back to God and made another request. "Lord, I know I asked you for a friend that was a Christian, but I don't like that one. We aren't compatible. I want to make another request. Can you take that one back and send me someone whom I will like, we will like the same kind of things, enjoy going to the same places, and enjoy being together?" Well, God tells us to make our request known to Him, so I did, and in His faithfulness, he soon took the other girl away and sent me Neesha.

Neesha and I were two peas in a pod until about her sophomore year in college where she went off to school and I was married and raising a family. Our lives became so different that we had entirely different experiences. I was proud of her life and more ashamed of my own and so soon we began communicating less and as the years passed, she and I both had substantial friend and life changes. One day I talked to God and said, "I want my best friend back!" He replied, "Go get her" (or something to that effect). I began calling her, reaching out often, remembering her, and began visiting her. Little by little with diligence and patience I gained my friends space back. I began to know her again as I had known her in the past. She was different but now I knew her in this new place as well as the old one.

God is beckoning you to receive and accept that you currently have; through His Son Jesus Christ and have always had a relationship with Him. You no longer have to be ashamed that life did not turn out the way you had wished and desired for it too. It is okay, He continues to hold you in His heart and is merely waiting for you to reach out again to find Him. May I encourage you to begin calling Him, reach out to him often, remember Him, and start visiting Him in prayer. You will know Him as He knows you.

THINK LIKE GOD REMINDERS

"Thou knowest my downsitting and mine uprising, thou understandest my thought afar off."
Psalm 139:2 KJV

Be comforted in knowing that the Creator of the Universe also created you and knows when you are sad, depressed, anxious, and in a storm. He is also aware of when you are scaling the mountain top. He is aware of you at all times. He sees you!

List two personal scriptures that God has given you about God *knowing* you:

1) _____
_____
_____
_____
_____

2) _____
_____
_____
_____
_____

What three steps will you take to implement the above scriptures?

1) _____
2) _____
3) _____

Chapter 2

JUST DO WHAT I SAY?

The next word we will explore is the word *"Commandment."* Now, how many of you just shuttered on the inside? Perhaps some of you just shuttered on the outside. I took a very unscientific survey using a small sample size and asked a question to see how others felt about the word commandment. My question was, "What is the first thing you think of when I say the word commandment? I got responses such as "rules, authority to give commands, something you have to do, laws, gotta do it right, order, consequences, and even 'sucka'! Most people who responded had a negative response or feeling toward the word. No one expressed it in its true glorious nature. I submit to you that this word will no longer be a hardship to you, but it will be a blessing that will change how you see God and how you receive what He has to say to you.

There are five different definitions for the word commandment. For this teaching, we will highlight only two of them. To understand what the writers of the Old Testament meant in their word choice let us go back to our dear friend, the SEC. We are referencing the word "commandment" that is used by God rather than man. This particular Old Testament description of 'commandment' found in the SEC as the word Mitsvâh/H4687 and from Sāwâ or

Tsâvâh/H6680. It means to command, order, **prescription**, and instruction.

In the New Testament, we see its sister word Entolē /G1781 which in the Greek is translated as, to command, give orders, give instruction, an authoritative **prescription**, a **precept**. According to Google dictionary, concerning the law; the word prescription defines as "the establishment of a claim founded on the basis of a long or indefinite period of uninterrupted use or of long-standing custom."

God's prescription shows us how God thinks and how He has always thought since before time began. He created, formed, and established the heavens and His kingdom based on this definite and long-standing way of thinking; which has resulted in His customs in which we are partakers. The word 'precept' means as "A command or principle intended especially as a general rule of action." The English Oxford dictionary defines it as "A way of regarding, understanding or interpreting something, a mental impression. Finally, the Merriam Webster defines it as "a rule that says how people should behave.

Additionally, the Greek word Entolē derives from two words one of which is "Telos" which translates by the SEC as: "end result, outcome, finish, goal." These definitions help us comprehend the finality of the way God thinks. He does not change His premise because we change ours, neither does He become wishy-washy. His first choice is also His last. His first and last thoughts concerning you are indefinite, lasting, and eternal.

God has been communicating with you since before the foundations of the world. He is not angry, hateful, or oblivious to you and your needs. He intentionally gave you His commandments so you would know how He perceives life. The word "commandment" translates to 'God's prescribed way of thinking.' In many cases, the word commandment is interchangeable with "word" and the "law" in both the old and new testament.

The best place to see where it begins is at the beginning. Let us look at Genesis, "And the Lord God took the man, and put him into the garden of Eden to dress it and to keep it. "And the Lord God commanded the man, saying, of every tree of the garden thou mayest freely eat: But of the tree of the knowledge of good and evil, thou shalt not eat of it: for in the day that thou eatest thereof thou shalt surely die" (Genesis 2:16-17). Have you ever wondered why Adam only had one commandment? Have you ever considered the tone in which God gave the command? I submit that He did not give the order in anger, violence, and wrath as some may think. It was not in a good/bad and right/wrong category as some have been taught; it was merely in the class of instruction, protection, and love.

I have had the honor of rea ring six children. Mia was the first. Her father and I would speak to her when she was still in my belly. We would have conversations with her as if she were already born and seemingly already in our arms. After only six weeks of maternity leave, I returned to work. I was sitting at my desk one day gazing at a picture of Mia. In this picture, she was about a month old. Her hair slicked down, her chubby cheeks and her pink pleated dress filled most of the picture frame. I loved her so much. I wanted the best for her. The best I could ever provide.

As my eyes began to fill with pride, admiration, and tears my breast filled too and started to leak. I went home that day, after being back at work for only about eight months; I looked at her father and said, "I'm putting in my two-week notice!" Although we worked opposite shifts, I just felt I had to be with her; protect, nurture, guide, and care for her with everything I had especially my time.

By the time she was waddling around the house, getting into everything she possibly could, I had already had her brother Asa. They were eleven months apart and quite the handful. Anyone who has done it knows that taking care of little people at any age is challenging, especially two little people at the same time.

One day the stove was glowing orange as I was preheating the oven for the evening meal. Our tiny three-bedroom house resembled a race track. You know, you could go to three different rooms just walking around in a circle. Watching my toddler go from room to room as I handled the other little one always had me on edge. As I changed my son's diaper, I looked up and saw Mia waddling her way to close to the stove for my comfort. "HOT!" I exclaimed in the sternest voice I could muster, instantly she stopped, possibly about five feet from the glowing stove, turned around, and started wailing. My intent was never to scare her. It was merely to warn her. Without much instruction, I wanted her to know she should avoid touching that hot stove. Although it was glowing, bringing warm comfort, and a new experience if she reached out for it, it could bring great pain.

With the understanding that we are handcrafted in God's image after His likeness and character, Genesis 1:26 (Tyndale, 1996) and that before we were in the belly of the womb, God knew us, had a plan for us, and He placed purpose for our lives in us before the foundations of the world. I propose that His instruction or commandment to Adam was that of a parent to a child who sees a bright hot stove for the first time. The warning is stern, firm, and loving. "HOT!" It is given swiftly, urgently, and with intensity to ensure the child understands and remembers "HOT." It is given with the heart and intent of the child never coming to any harm. It is said so that the child understands the severity of the situation and can still admire the beautiful warm glow from afar.

Adam had no earthly parents or what we consider a childhood. He was placed in the garden of Eden as an adult and given immediate responsibilities and assignments. Therefore, his loving heavenly Father simply gave a wise and precautious instruction as needed. The same way He speaks to us in a still small voice He talked to Adam. The sound was tender and true, explaining very little but protecting him and providing safety. It was not a command that scolded him on the hand or the backside. No, it was tender and firm, ensuring Adam understood the responsibility and severity of the situation. However, why was there a commandment in the first place?

Without the commandment or in other words, without God's prescribed way of thinking, Adam would not have been given a choice. That was one of the first gifts God gave man. The power of choice. Humankind was to use this gift to love and obey God utilizing man's own free will--his soul. For humanity to choose to say, "yes Lord I want to serve and love you." Alternatively, for a man to choose to say "no, this is my life and even if you gave it to me, I decide to live it my way." With either decision, it was a decision mankind could make.

God is so amazing and displays such amazing love toward us that even though He made us to demonstrate His character and govern the earth on His behalf, He still allowed the man a choice. A choice to serve Him or not serve Him. An opportunity to love Him or not love Him. A decision to obey Him or not obey Him. Not just because He is our God, King, and Creator, but because we choose Him.

Without giving Adam one command, Adam never would have had a free will. The one commandment ascribed to man in the garden of Eden is as follows: "But of the tree of the knowledge of good and evil, thou shalt not eat of it: for in the day that thou eatest thereof thou shalt surely die." This one commandment was given and designed for three things; (1) to give the power of choice, (2) provide protection, and (3) to teach Adam how God thinks. God was essentially saying to Adam, 'you are not designed to handle the knowledge of good and evil.' The heart of God was conveying to Adam, with too much knowledge you will surely die.

When we tell our children, the stove is hot we do not immediately explain in these terms: "son, do you see the glowing orange light, that is called fire or heat. If you at any time touch the stove while that fire or heat has been on for any length of time, it will burn your fingers. Son, I know you do not know what burn is, but it is uncomfortable, can cause severe damage, and may cause you to go to the hospital. At any rate, it will inflict great pain." Do we give full disclosure when we see emanate danger? No, generally we give out the loudest, quickest, and the sharpest warning to ensure our loved one is safe. We want our children to know the danger that precedes them, just like God conveyed to Adam. He wanted Adam to understand the way He thought. God wanted to teach Adam to think and reason like his Creator while using his own free will. God wanted Adam to display the character and image He had put in him. For Adam to do this, he had to understand how God thinks.

The "commandment," or "word," or "law" of God is God's prescribed way of thinking. It allows a man to know or remember how God thinks. Once humanity opposes God's command, word, or law he decides to think or reason another way. Humankind chooses to reason in ways that resist the way of God reasoning. He concludes his way, idea, and thoughts are superior to God's.

After humankind opposed God's way of thinking or broke the command, God had to institute hundreds of commandments so we could know and understand the mind of God. God wanted humanity to understand His prescribed way of thinking. Since God's thoughts are not the thoughts of man and his ideas are not the ways of mere men than it was necessary to express to humanity explicitly what God's thoughts were and are. Humankind is designed to rule in the earth as it is in heaven. Humanity, to fulfill this mandate, had to know what to implement and what systems to utilize in the world. Therefore, humankind needed instructions (1) to make wise decisions, (2) provide protection to those in the earth, and (3) to spread a culture of God's way of thinking.

God's commandments, word, or law is not religious nor is it a religion. The commandments of God show us how God thinks. Let us review some scriptures to illustrate my point. In Genesis 26:1-5 God instructs, prophesies, and gives reason over His servant Isaac and said, "Because that Abraham obeyed my voice, and kept my charge, my commandments, my statues, and my laws." Now paraphrasing: "Because that Abraham obeyed my voice, and kept my charge, *my prescribed way of thinking*, my statues, and my laws."

Deuteronomy 4:40 says, "Thou shalt keep therefore his statutes, and his commandments, which I command thee this day, that it may go well with thee, and with thy children after thee, and that thou mayest prolong thy days upon the earth, which the Lord thy God giveth thee, forever." Evaluate it this way. "Thou shalt keep therefore his statues, *and God's way of thinking*, which I charge thee this day, that it may go well with thee, and with thy children after thee, and that thou mayest prolong thy days upon the earth, which the Lord thy God giveth thee, forever. Here is our last one. "I am a stranger in the earth: hide not thy commandments from me." Psalm 119:19 thus, I am a stranger in the earth: hide not *God's prescribed way of thinking* from me.

God is showing us that his commandments are not grievous; (1 John 5:3) and this is the love of God that we keep *His prescribed way of thinking* thus his commandments. By obeying His commands, we express we love God and man. Following after God's commandment or His prescribed way of thinking is not that difficult. It was never designed to be something we could not relate to or obtain. It was not established to push us around and make us go here and do this or that.

No, my friend, it is designed to give you such peace and align you with your Creator. It predestines you that as you live your life on this earth, you can see the plans and purposes of God for your life and your community. His commandments, word, and law were given to you so that you could recognize His voice, His passions, His character, and remind you that you already *knew* Him before the foundations of the world. Although you may not remember that all of the time, if you go back to His prescribed way of thinking, it will lead you back to those truths and you will obtain peace, grace, power, and strength to endure.

No matter how hard it gets, that strength to endure can pull you through. The scriptures state it this way: "He gives power to the weak, And to those who have no might He increases strength. Even the youth shall faint and be weary, And the young men shall utterly fall, but those who wait on the Lord shall renew their strength; they shall mount up with wings as eagles, they shall run and not be weary, they shall walk and not faint" (Isaiah 40:29-31 NKJV).

Due to an unhealthy introduction to sexuality at an early age, my misplaced desire to express my feelings as a youth left me in a precarious position. When I was a preteen, I was in love with the "boy next door" who was about my age. We had been friends for a while when one summer, we began to spend much of our time together playing ATARI® video games. It was captivating and compelling. His house, my house, back and forth, gaming for hours at a time. The more time we spent with each other, the more I wanted to share all of my passions, expressions, and love for him.

One day while on the telephone I decided he would come over the next day and we would copulate. Although I had never copulated before I knew he was the person I would spend the rest of my life with, so it was okay. I prepared for the occasion as much as possible. I made sure I was clean, wore a short blue jean skirt, and even put on a pair of my father's girlfriends blue tie string panties that tied on the sides.

He came over, and we got right to it. The problem was I was so young and inexperienced, he was so naive and excited that our entire encounter lasted for about ten seconds. Within those ten seconds, there had been a release and a knock on the front door. Since we were in the living room, he was scared half to death, ran down the hallway to the bathroom, and swiftly shut the door.

About three or four months later after my thirteenth birthday I found out I was pregnant. I was devastated. My inquisitive experiment and the self-discovery of my body was now the most publicly humiliating outward expression I had ever encountered. I had a small frame and so when the other eighth grade girls began to ask me was I pregnant I was horrified.

No matter what I wore, I could not hide the fact that day by day I was getting bigger and bigger. No matter how I insisted in my mind this was not real, and that this was not genuinely happening, no matter how many ways I crafted a plan of denial my body screamed the truth to all who saw me. I felt so judged, so defeated. I wanted to take my life. I did not want to go to hell. After the incident at school with the girls asking me was I pregnant I wanted more than ever to take my life. How in the world could I go on? How in the world could I face my family, friends, and classmates? How could I ever look myself in the eyes and see beauty ever again?

One night before going to bed I decided I would do what I had to do. I would take my own life. I wanted it to be fast, effective, and definite. I went into the bathroom, opened the medicine cabinet and scanned each shelf for the most potent medicine I could find. The result happened to be Tylenol® in the capsules. I took them out of the cabinet and laid them out in a row. "How can I be sure this will work?" I thought. "I know, I will take them out of the capsules and just take it straight."

As I washed the grainy particles down with the water from the bathroom sink, it burned my throat to no end. I went to bed, slept, woke up the next morning with a burning sore throat and decided, "I guess that is not the route for me." A few weeks later my family had made provisions for me to leave my school and to reside at a temporary home for unwed mothers until the baby arrived. I would finish out my eighth-grade year there, make new friends there, and bring a new life into the world there.

There is never any need to make a permanent decision to take your own life. Your life, forever hidden in Him, gives you the key to connect and embrace His purpose. When you feel defeated and that you cannot go on, remember that God has already thought about and planned for everything that you have encountered, and He has also prescribed a solution.

God knew before the foundations of the world that I would bring a life into the world at a very young age. He knew of my fears, depression, and shame. The Father had already prepared a way of escape for me. He had a path of righteousness already outlined for me. At the time, I had no idea there was such a thing as a home for unwed mothers. I had no idea anyone I knew would soon learn of the resource and would be able to connect me; however, God knew! I just went along with His prescribed way of thinking for the current situation. My solution was already cultivated in my blueprint before the world began. It was one of many paths already orchestrated for my life.

How will you find your solution? Go to His word. Read it as if you are looking for His way of thinking and that you understand His way is infinite! It always has and will still work. He has a purpose for you that was designed and blueprinted before you ever got here. Sometimes life can be so heavy and hurt so badly. The death of a loved one, a divorce, loss of a career/employment, a family member commits suicide. The pressures of this world can influence us to a point we become stagnate in our emotions, mind, and heart. However, He is our strength!

The strength of the Lord outlined in Isaiah 40:29 refers to power, might, ability, often physical strength and the vigor of good health. It references a lizard, and not just any lizard but a chameleon. The undergirding that God has for you gives you power, ability, physical force, and good health which includes good mental and spiritual health. When I went to the home for unwed mothers, I was released from my current pressures. I was able to read my bible, pray, befriend and minister God's love to other young women who found themselves in the same place for various reasons. I was in the process of waiting upon the Lord. Sometimes you too will be required to wait upon the Lord during your time of grief or loss.

Not to absently wait but waiting on the Lord in an expectation that He will be there to deliver you, to gather you to Himself. As the chameleon can hide and blend in with his surroundings, so will you be sheltered while you are waiting.

There is a special grace that comes to those who are waiting upon the Lord especially during a loss. Psalms 91:9-16 NLT says it this way: "If you make the Lord your refuge if you make the Most High your shelter; no evil will conquer you; no plague will come near your dwelling, For he orders his angels to protect you wherever you go. They shall hold you with their hands to keep you from striking your foot on a stone. You will trample down lions and poisonous snakes; you will crush fierce lions and serpents under your feet! The Lord says, "I will rescue those who love me, I will protect those who trust in my name. When they call on me, I will answer; I will be with them in trouble, I will rescue them and honor them. I will satisfy them with a long life and give them my salvation."

You may be wondering by now why I use the word 'prescribe' when labeling God's way of thinking. Exploring that for a moment, according to Merriam-Webster dictionary one of the definitions for 'prescribe' is "to lay down a guide, direction, or rule of action: to specify with authority, to designate or order the use of as a remedy." It is also a synonym for; you guessed it 'command.' To prescribe is to write, be listed or to be recorded. It is what happened when God wrote out the commandments on the stone tablets given to Moses for the Israelites. He was declaring to them His way of thinking that would lead and guide them into all truth. His prescribed way of thinking would give them direction and would remedy their problems, concerns, and questions. He was showing them that his way of thinking was an established authority that once set, could never be overturned by anyone but Himself. It was/is the highest authority because it was/is the first and last word, idea, commandment, law ever declared, spoken and even written from God into the earth.

Since He *knew* you before you were even formed in the belly His blueprint for you stated, indicated, and desired His way of thinking to be written upon the tablet of your heart. He gives reference to it in Jeremiah 31:31-37 for our intended purpose we will review one verse although I encourage you to read all seven scripture references. Verse thirty-three from the NLT says, "But this is the new covenant I will make with the people of Israel on that day, says the Lord. I will put my laws in their minds, and I will write them on their hearts. I will be their God, and they will be my people." God is telling us that His prescribed way of thinking will be written on our hearts and established in our minds. His prescribed (direction and written/spoken word that guides) way of thinking has authority and power and thrives forever.

THINK LIKE GOD REMINDERS

"I opened my mouth and panted: for I longed for thy commandments." Psalms 119:131 KJV

Desire God's prescribed way of thinking more than water by allowing His words to penetrate your heart and change your mind.

List two personal scriptures that God has given you about *commandment* or His prescribed way of thinking:

1) _____
_____
_____
_____
_____

2) _____
_____
_____
_____
_____

What three steps will you take to implement the above scriptures?

1) _____
2) _____
3) _____

Chapter 3
SIN, IT IS NOT WHAT YOU THINK

Before we get started, I want you to quickly grab a piece of paper or type the answer in your phone. Before you proceed any further, jot down the first three things that come to mind when you hear the word sin. As the next word for exploration the definition you will come to know may be tough to digest. It tends to be harder to comprehend because our Adversary uses it as a means to keep us in bondage through our thinking. Let me encourage you that as you read this chapter, you may need to take a few deep breaths. You may need to stop after reading only a few pages to gather your thoughts. That is expected and acceptable. I ask that you do not reject the word (or the law, thus his prescribed way of thinking). The definition you will find in the upcoming pages may look very different from your own. Be willing to expand the way you think and consider the truth that unfolds before you.

For explanation purposes, I want to note which definitions we are using in this teaching to survey *sin*. Using the SEC, the Old Testament word sin I am describing is called Hātā/H2398 and means: 'to do wrong; to willfully act contrary to the will and law of God.' In Greek it is Hamartia/G266 and means "wrongdoing, usually an act contrary to the will and law of God." I want to take this time to emphasize two words found within each definition. The words law and will.

If you remember from our previous chapters, the word command/commandment can be interchangeable with the word "law" and "word" in many cases. In this definition, we will be interchanging the word law for the phrase, God's prescribed way of thinking. Therefore, the literal definition begins to unveil for us. Sin is willfully acting contrary to the will of God and His prescribed way of thinking. Since thoughts come before actions, the authors' definition of sin summarizes as follows: "Sin is willfully thinking in a way that opposes the way God thinks which leads to actions that oppose the desires, purposes, nature, and plans of God."

Will or Thelō/G2309 defines in the SEC as: to will, decide, want to, to desire. We can bring our definition to a final close here. "Sin is to join your will to think in a way that opposes the way God thinks which leads to actions that oppose the desires, purposes, nature, and plans of God." Now, look at your paper or phone. What did you list? Did it resemble the exploration above? If not, I implore you to continue reading. You have received the wrong bill of goods. You are perhaps living your life via a misinterpreted periscope.

Understanding the meaning of a thing can open up truth you would have never found otherwise. John 8:32 says it best, "And ye shall know the truth, and the truth shall make you free." Freedom comes when you have the truth and with the truth comes wisdom and understanding. The writer of Proverbs 4:7 put it this way, "Wisdom is the principal thing; therefore, get wisdom: and with all thy getting get understanding." Here is probably an appropriate place to take a deep breath. This understanding is a new concept to many of you.

Sin itself is not the list of all the wrong things, habits, and desires you possibly listed on your paper/phone. Sin itself is to willfully think in a way that is contrary to the way God thinks. As a result, to thinking this way, you kindle the fire of desire, and eventually, it builds up to actions that produce the fruit of which you may have listed on your paper/phone (James 1:14-15).

During my first marriage, I experienced financial mistreatment. Mostly due to each of our cultural way of thinking. We established our home out of a spectrum of gender roles and unspoken ideologies. We had our perceptions about what each of us should do as a spouse. We were a young couple married at nineteen and twenty-one. We did not consult the scriptures to see if our thoughts and desires aligned with God's way of thinking, we just did what each of us thought was right and best in our own eyes. Eventually, our last child had come, and in both of our minds, she was the final melon. However, neither of us took any measures to ensure that she would be the caboose.

At the time we owned a minivan. It was an eight-seater and already filled to capacity. One day I took a pregnancy test and my worst fear was confirmed. I was pregnant. It should have been a time of rejoicing, but it was not! Instead, it was a time of gloom and tension as my husband paced back and forth looking almost sickly. I quickly made up in my mind that I had to have an abortion. The ironic thing was I would never have guessed in a million years that I would come to this conclusion. I was raised to know and believe that abortion was against the will of God. It was a value I held close to my heart. I had birthed out seven times because of this conviction.

This time I felt I was stuck. I felt trapped. Everyday my thoughts continued to say: "If you have another baby, where in the world would you put him in that van?" I decided I had to get the abortion. In my reasoning I had no other options. I had the conversation with my husband; his response was "okay if that is what you want to do." I loathed that response with every fiber of my being. I wanted him to say, "Girl are you crazy, it's not that bad! We will get through this somehow." That, however, was not the case. Consequently, I made the appointment, got the abortion, and went before my pastors the next day to confess my sin, seek help, and the face of God. Something was seriously wrong.

I may take slack for this, but I challenge you that the initial *sin* was not the abortion. The abortion was the consequence of the original sin which was my thinking, "Where in the world would I put another child in that van?" That way of thinking did not bring forth fruits of righteousness, quite the opposite it brought forth death. My thinking led me down a path of unrighteousness because I refused to line up my thoughts with His word.

At the time, I refused to read my bible. I knew God would bring conviction to my heart if I allowed His word to penetrate it. I knew if I would confess my faults and repent (which means to change your thoughts, attitudes, and behaviors) and be converted (which means to change your actions/intentions) then God would bring about a different result. Since I could not see what the result would be, at that moment, I refused to believe God. I willfully joined my thoughts to a way that opposed the way God thinks which led to actions that oppose the desires of God's purpose. God saw my sin in my thoughts long before an act took place!

I could have gone to God's word (or his prescribed way of thinking) and declared that His word was/is always right. I could have taken the truth unto my bosom and fortified a strong blueprinted pathway. I could have chosen to "Buy the truth, and sell it not; also, wisdom, instruction, and understanding" (Proverbs 23:23). You see this scripture here gives me all that I need. It tells me to hold on to what God is thinking. God is the truth! He is telling me here not to consider my surroundings but to hold on to this truth like it is pure gold and not sell it or forfeit what I have for any price. His way of thinking says if I hold the truth, it will cause me to have wisdom, instruction, and understanding.

Simply put, God would reveal Himself to me for another child, and it had already been mapped out in my blueprint before the world began. I did not wait upon the Lord. I did not choose to allow Him to renew my strength. I did not consider that His way was the best way all the time and for that, I suffered scar tissue in my physical body. Dear friends, God's way of thinking is always the best way. It brings us into a full and healthy place perpetually.

There is a couple in the bible, they were brilliant, healthy, teachable, attentive, and owned it all. You are right if you were thinking of Adam and Eve. The most remarkable persons ever created, filled with brilliance and vigor yet they did not take responsibility for steering their way of thinking. Let us review some details in their lives that I feel are still beneficial for us to acknowledge today.

Chapter three of the book of Genesis opens with the serpent, whom Satan had infiltrated conferring a new idea to Eve. He questioned Eve about what command God had given to her and Adam. He inquired of Eve about God's prescribed way of thinking. He begins to challenge her thoughts as he throws out questions that he and she already knew the answers. The Life Application translation says it this way: "Did God really say you must not eat any of the fruit in the garden?" Innocently enough her response was genuine and earnest. "Of course, we may eat it. It's only the fruit from the tree at the center of the garden that we are not allowed to eat. God says we must not eat it or even touch it, or we will die." Eve knew and stated the truth. Unfortunately, she did not buy it and sell it not! Instead, we find that sin enters the picture.

The same opposition Satan had in the heavens to the Father, he now releases it in the earth expressing his thoughts. He replies to Eve, "You won't die! God knows that your eyes will be open when you eat it. You will become just like God, knowing everything both good and evil." The sin in Genesis chapter three began as Eve began to consider Satan's thoughts and allowed her will to agree with Satan's way of thinking. She was supposed to reject the thought, go back to the precious truth she had, and not sell it for anything in the world. She was supposed to say, "Your wrong and God's way of thinking is right! I will not touch nor eat of the fruit of that tree because that is how God thinks about it.

After Eve considered Satan's ideas, or sin, and thoughts that opposed the way God thought; which led to actions that oppose the desires, purpose, nature, and plans of God; then she received in her soul the opposite way of thinking as a truth that was above God's thoughts. Next, in verse six of the same translation, it reveals, "The woman was convinced. The fruit that looked so fresh and delicious would make her so wise! So, she ate some of the fruit. She also gave some to her husband who was with her. Then he ate it too" (Genesis 3:4-6 NLT). The woman was convinced, and although she had not eaten the fruit, yet the sin happened when she was 'convinced.' In her mind, she decided that the instruction God gave was not entirely the best thing for her. She relied on her senses to guide her. The fruit appealed to her eyes and in her perception, would make her wise.

Eve did not stop and consider that she was already wise. She did not bother to remember all of the other fruit in the garden provided for food and that was delightful to view. She negated reflecting on the truth that she was already a god because she was made in God's image after his likeness (Gen. 1:26). Neither did she review what God had initially told she and her husband. Without inquiring of God 'is there a reason we should not eat of the tree?' Eve did not take responsibility for her thoughts and thus her actions. Instead, she rehearsed in her mind all the perceived benefits Satan had placed before her.

The temptation Satan brought to Adam and Eve was the temptation of thinking independently from God. The sin was conceived in her heart when she considered the idea long enough to be 'convinced.' She aligned her thoughts, mind, and will to agree with the word the Adversary had given her. Satan does us the same way today. He convinces us with his influence that God's way could not possibly work for us! We have been trained culturally to be, work, and sometimes play independently from others and especially our parents. Satan, the god of this world influences us (2 Cor. 4:4) to think like, act like, and live like those who do not know the salvation experience found in Christ Jesus.

He tempts us just like he did Adam and Eve so long ago. He influences us in the realm we believe the most, in our thoughts. Not only do we accept our views the most, but we are also a combined make up of what we think. Proverbs 23:7 shows us God's way of thinking, "For as he thinketh in his heart, so is he…" What we think tells us and the world who we are. Our thinking instantaneously determines our position, whether we are operating in the kingdom or operating in the earth. Whether we are walking in the spirit or being subject to the work of the flesh; our thoughts and what we join them to determine which vein of the blueprint we will take; which paths we agree to walk on.

What have you been thinking about lately? When your thoughts do not agree with the way God thinks, do you quickly catch the idea and proceed to follow God's prescribed way of thinking instead by, "casting down imagination and every high thing that exalteth itself against the knowledge of God and bringing into captivity every thought to the obedience of Christ; and having in a readiness to revenge all disobedience when your obedience is fulfilled" (2 Cor. 10:5-6)? You have the power, authority, and right to do just that!

Cast down your imaginations that deny you the right to do what God is saying you can and should do because it is best for you. Once you realize that is what you are listening to, counter it with the truth! Say out loud as Paul did, "I find that the strength of Christ's explosive power infuses me to conquer every difficulty (Phil. 4:13 TPT). If you hear in your mind, you are stupid; catch that thought and throw it down on the floor. Say with a stern voice, "I have the mind of Christ," so I am brilliant, 1 Cor. 2:16 (Nelson, 1990). Perhaps you hear inside, I am all alone, and no one loves me. Once you realize your mind is drifting and replaying those words over and over, buy the truth and sell it not. Instead say, …"for he hath said, I will never leave thee, nor forsake thee" (Heb. 13:5 KJV) and John 3:16 which says, "For God so loved the world that He gave His only begotten Son that whosoever believeth in Him should not perish but have everlasting life."

THINK LIKE GOD REMINDERS

"I give all my thanks to God, for his mighty power has finally provided a way out through our Lord Jesus, the Anointed One! So, if left to myself, the flesh is aligned with the law of sin, but now my renewed mind is fixed on and submitted to God's righteous principles.   Romans 7:25 TPT

As a born-again believer, you are no longer bound to thinking against the way God thinks. Through the blood of Jesus, you have a new mind and are able to think just like God each day.

List two personal scriptures that God has given you about freedom from *sin*:

1) _____
_____
_____
_____
_____

2) _____
_____
_____
_____
_____

What three steps will you take to implement the above scriptures?

1) _____
2) _____
3) _____

Chapter 4
BELIEVE, OR UNBELIEF YOU DECIDE

Our next word to explore here is *unbelief*. Unbelief is a powerful word. On the surface, it appears as if the person who has disbelief does not believe God. They cannot accept what God says is true. However, that is not the totality of the meaning. We will look at that for a moment.

The word unbelief is found only sixteen times and just in the new testament in the KJV of the bible. It has only two meanings. One meaning is from SEC Apeitheia/G543, and it translates as disobedience. The second meaning is what I want to expound upon here called Apistia/G570. SEC defines it as "lack of faith; often with the implication of stubbornly refusing to believe or act in accordance with God's will or law." In essence, *unbelief* is ironically mirrored to sin. If you recall, "Sin is willfully thinking in a way that opposes the way God thinks which leads to actions that oppose the desires, purpose, and plans of God." Therefore, unbelief is to stubbornly refuse to believe and act in agreement with Gods prescribed way of thinking, His desires, purposes, and plans.

When you refuse to believe God you essentially say, "I intentionally, willfully, reject what God has placed before me. I intentionally, willfully, reject the way God thinks, His desires, purpose, and plans for my life." When you exercise your power of choice to believe God or not believe (unbelief) God you are a mighty force. A force one way or the other, to be reckoned with by others.

When Adam and Eve made the fatal decision to disbelieve by agreeing to eat of the tree of the knowledge of good and evil, it changed the course of their lives and the lives of humanity forever. When the children of Israel faced the opportunity to enter the promised land that God had sworn, He would give them; the only thing that stopped them from entering in was their unbelief (Numbers Chapter 14). Unfortunately, they reaped forty years in the desert, and only two of the elders of that generation got to enter in because of their belief, and God brought the Israelites children into the land flowing with milk and honey instead of their parents.

A year or so after I had my very first child, I received a prophetic word from a prophetess of God. This renown prophetess in our community was a good friend of my foster family. The power of God moved in her life just like it did in the book of Acts and the days of old. She had seen food multiply in her kitchen while she was stirring the meat. She had believed God and seen Him fill up her gas tank as she and her husband watched the needle hand move from empty to full. She had encountered witches, warlocks, demon possessed people and had seen them set free by the power of God.

She had gone into the streets of her neighborhood while gang violence and drug dealing were taking place and commanded all ungodly activity to cease, it did. Later when I became part of her ministry, I too became an eye witness to many miracles including seeing limbs grow right before our eyes. I give you this background to establish the soundness of the prophetic move in her life and the consecrated life she lived and continues to live.

The prophetic word she had given me when I was around the age of fourteen or so was that God had restored my body like a virgin. Now there was no test I could have taken to validate if the word was correct except that the anointing of God upon her life confirmed the words from her mouth. I would have to accept it by faith.

It was a hard saying for me to grasp. Although I wanted it to be true because I did not believe God swiftly by buying the truth and selling it not; instead I experienced the parable of the sower. Matthew 13:19 plainly states what happened to me. When I heard the word of truth from the kingdom, because I did not understand it nor continue to seek God about it, my adversary came and stole the truth sown in my heart. It was evident as years later I copulated before I was married. If I had held on to the precious gift God had restored to me, I would never have let it go before the designated time.

Sometimes we think that we have a right to refuse stubbornly to accept God's prescribed way of thinking. I am not saying we do not have a choice because we do. However, in doing so, we are fighting against the truth and rebelling against our deliverer. We consider the options placed on the table and conclude "the way we think about the situation is better than the way God reasons." Frankly, we find our way of thinking is better than anyone else's at the time. We relentlessly fight against the truth to our detriment. Often after all has gone wrong, we turn and blame God for the imbalance in our lives.

Another form of stubbornly refusing to accept God's way of thinking that is appealing to large numbers today is the idea that "Since we are not hurting anyone, it is acceptable not to believe there is a God." That statement is a lie. That form of thinking hurts our neighbors and ourselves. Those who are believers of Christ and have received him into their hearts by confessing with their mouth that Jesus is Lord and believe in their heart that God raised him from the dead, (Romans 10:9 NLT) now partner with God to fulfill his will in the earth.

His will includes a believer feeding, clothing, and giving to others. To stop oppression and to help family members in need and not hide from them (Isaiah 58:6-8). He asks us to love our enemies to completely display in the earth how God thinks and acts (Matthew 5:43-48). When God says for us to leave our job, move to another state, give away a precious item we own; we openly, hastily reject it because it is not what we want to do. We do not understand it, neither do we take the time to go back to Him and continue to dialogue about it until we can say yes in our hearts.

However, if we as believers obey, then once we leave that job, we release it to the person whom God has appointed to be there in this season. Once we move, our property is now open for the person who has been praying about their next home in our old neighborhood, at the price they can afford. When we give away that item that we wanted to hold onto and help those in need, then people are cared for, and God is glorified. Yes, we hurt others when we do not believe there is a God.

We are intrinsically and uniquely joined one to another. Believers are mandated to connect to this universe and each other in a way that causes us to thrive not just survive. Just like the plants on earth need us to help cultivate and maintain a conducive environment for growth, we need those same plants to in turn give us oxygen to allow us to breathe and to provide food. Each person on this earth needs another person. When we are in college, we need others to teach us and others to help us study for classes. We need someone every now and again to come along and encourage us. Sometimes we need others to provide shelter or to feed us.

If we do not believe there is a God, we will not be agents of change. Negating to lend a listening ear to our creator to find out how we can serve our neighbor. When we find ourselves in need, we will not be a recipient of anything because we will have accepted a lie to be the truth, "no one is, can, or wants to help you."

Scriptures relate it best "...Believe in the Lord your God so shall ye be established; believe his prophets, so shall ye prosper (2 Chronicles 20:20 KJV). "They replied, believe in the Lord Jesus, and you will be saved-you and your household" (Acts 16:31). "So, you see, it is impossible to please God without faith. Anyone who wants to come to him must believe that there is a God and that he rewards those who sincerely seek him (Hebrews 11:6 NLT). Plainly stated, believing in God causes you to be established, rescued from all things that bind you and your family, and brings you into rewards set aside for you since before the foundations of the world.

I am unsure of your stance, but I want it to be said of me just like it was said of Abram in Genesis 15:6, 'she believed God and the Lord accounts it to her for righteousness sake.' I want my practice of belief to credit to my account with God. I have seen God do amazing things in my life when I intentionally decide to believe him. As unbelief is; to stubbornly refuse to accept what God is saying; belief is to willfully acknowledge what God is saying and agree with it.

Maybe that sounded a little too easy, but it is in fact, that easy! If you struggle with believing God, you never have to wrestle again. How do you believe God? AGREE WITH WHAT HE SAYS. If it is a hard saying that you cannot quite wrap your mind around or you are void of understanding; agree with what He says. If it looks impossible; agree with what He says. If you do not want to do it, agree with what He says and then accept His prescribed way of thinking and ask Him to work in you both to will and to do of His good pleasure Philippians 2:13 (Tyndale, 1996).

When Christ redeemed you by His blood and made you acceptable to the Father again, the covenant He made with you stated he would deliver you from all bondage. Unbelief is strict bondage. It causes you not to receive the precious promises of God. Negating you of your inherent promises and blessings. Smothering your ideas, creativity, and freedom. Agreeing with unbelief causes automatic defeat in your endeavors without even knowing why.

Defeat does not have to apply to you. I charge you just as Jehoshaphat charged the children of Judah and the inhabitants of Jerusalem. "Believe in the Lord your God, so shall ye be established;

believe in his prophets, so shall ye prosper" (2 Chron. 20:20 KJV). You will no longer be in lack due to your unbelief. No longer in bondage because you stubbornly refuse to accept God's prescribed way of thinking. No, you have the truth, and you will receive it. Even if you have to go back and talk to God about your challenges you will not dismiss the truth! You will agree with God. You will say yes Lord you are right! I believe; help thou mine unbelief (Mark 9:24). If you do not believe God, yet you are wise enough to admit your disbelief and request for Him to help you in that area, He is bound by the salvation clause to deliver you, rescue you, and help you so that you can believe Him. He wants you to prosper and to obtain success! He is on your side.

    When God began to minister to me about the unbelief in my own heart, He did so before he explained this truth to me. In other words, I started to experience the truth; then He visually explained what was happening. Although I was challenged with a divorce years ago, God restored me and placed a fantastic partner in my life. My husband and I had recently gotten married and were on a strict plan to become debt free. In a matter of six months, we had paid off all credit card debt and one vehicle which came to about seventeen thousand dollars. We were on an aggressive plan that would have the rest of our debt of about fifty thousand dollars paid in full within the next fourteen months.

    We continued to seek God for His best plan to pay off the debt. Finally, we were sure we had the outline figured out and then something unexpected was placed on the table. My husband and I wanted to start our own consulting business, but due to the demand of our time-consuming jobs, we only picked at our entrepreneurship here and there. One day my husband presented the concept of me leaving my place of employment to pursue our business agenda. After several months we felt it was time to make a move. I was leaving a job making a very healthy income and a developing career, to pursue something I was not sure would flourish.

When you believe God, several things begin to take place. Better health, creativity, open passageways, and your purpose manifests. My employment involved much walking, so I was getting in over my scheduled ten thousand steps each day which positively contributed to my physical health. The nature of my employment was mentally challenging however, once I came home, I began to see a positive change in my mental health as well. I was calmer, less anxious, and began to think more clearly than I could ever remember thinking before.

I came from a very creative family but had never felt I was very creative. My family consists of bakers, hair stylist, artist, poets, musicians, teachers, writers, gardeners, and seamstress's. I felt I had very little of these talents and the ones I recognized only showed up every once in a while, with minimal skill. When I came home, my creativity level shot up probably fifty percent. I see it flourishing more and more as the days extend.

I have seen passageways open. An exchange of ideas, businesses have been crafted, volunteer opportunities fulfilled, and more plans are on the horizon. My spouse's relationship with the

Father has increased. Moreover, how my husband hears the Lord has been growing, the voice of the Lord has been distinct, clear, and daily. You may wonder what his relationship with God has to do with me coming home. Well you see, he was blessed. It brought a release to him that he could not have experienced if I had not resigned from my employment. You never know what act of obedience and belief will create God's favor on your life.

Ultimately, the purposes of our lives have been made manifest. Every month there is something else. We see more of the vision for our marriage, God has revealed some ministry efforts we will undertake, and we are moving from one state to another state; making plans as of this writing. The act of trusting God includes moving from an area that we have spent a majority of our lives (for me all of my life) into a region that we know little about and without knowing anyone there. Leaving that which is familiar, our children, family, and friends; is all a part of God's purpose for our lives as we trust him. Some of the vision is abstract, but some of it is intentional and explicit.

Believing God came when my husband and I agreed with what God said. We did not challenge it. We did not say "well we have this debt free plan, so we do not think this is a good time Lord." Instead, we agreed with His prescribed way of thinking and began to see our lives change right in front of our eyes. You too can believe God even if you have never done it before.

In agreeing with how God thinks, you automatically open yourself to God's kingdom. You will no longer be a religious person having ritualized ideas that run your life no matter what the Spirit of the Lord says. You will be a person who is led by the Spirit of God, freely moving and living and being. His ideas and not your own will motivate you. You will submit your thinking to His will, and in doing so, your desires will produce acts of righteousness. These righteous acts will then produce life everlasting.

THINK LIKE GOD REMINDERS

"I believed, therefore have I spoken I was greatly afflicted."
Psalm 116:10 KJV

"Even when it seems I'm surrounded by many liars and my own fears, and though I'm hurting in my suffering and trauma, I still stay faithful to God and speak words of faith.
Psalm 116:10-11 TPT

It is important to say aloud what you believe. Take the truths you have understood that align themselves with God's way of thinking and say them boldly, loudly, audibly, and often.

List two personal scriptures that God has given you about *belief*:

1) _____
_____
_____
_____
_____

2) _____
_____
_____
_____
_____

What three steps will you take to implement the above scriptures?

1) _____
2) _____
3) _____

Chapter 5
REPENT, YOU WILL BE GLAD YOU DID

Our final word is repent. Oddly enough repentance is not going before an entire body of people, publicly confessing your sins. It is not repeatedly rehearsing all of the wrong things you have done and then begging God to forgive you. Neither is it subjecting yourself to all manner of cutting, whipping or any other forms of self-mutilation to show God you are sorry for the wrong you have done in your life.

Here I will present our next word in three forms, Repent, Repented, and Repentance as taken from the New Testament. The SEC defines them as such: Repent/G3340-Metanoeō and means "to change any/all of the elements composing one's life. Thoughts, attitudes, behaviors concerning the demands of God for right living." Repented/G3338-Metalelomai and means "to regret, changed of mind, and remorseful." Then we have repentance/G3341-Metanoia which means "a change of mind. The state of changing any or all of the element's composing one's life: thoughts, attitudes, behaviors concerning the demands of God for right living. Which refers to foundational salvation and ongoing repentance in the Christian life."

Plainly stated to repent means to change your thoughts, attitudes, and behaviors to align themselves with God's prescribed way of thinking. In doing so, it transforms all of the elements composing one's life.

Notice the definition does not resemble any form of public confessions, repetitive self-bashing, or self-mutilation. Please do not misunderstand me; there is a place for admission. The scriptures do encourage us to "confess your faults one to another, and pray one for another, that ye may be healed." "The effectual fervent prayer of a righteous man availeth much" (James 5:16 KJV). Another scripture also reads ", therefore, whosoever shall confess me before men, him will I also confess before my Father which is in heaven" (Matthew 10:32).

Neither of these scriptures is referencing the definition of repent or its variances stated above. I believe it is essential to make a public display of your confession to Christ Jesus by receiving Him in your heart and confessing that He is now Lord of your life. Going before a body of believers and acknowledging this accepted change is an admirable ceremony. I merely want to outline the difference between that ceremony and the definition of repentance.

If repentance was something that you did while watching your television and you were the only one there, then you should call someone or tell a friend or neighbor. An open expression and confession are public signs that you honor, respect, and are not ashamed of your new-found relationship with Christ Jesus, and He declares to honor you before His Father likewise. When we confess our faults before others in the above scriptural context, we do so to take ownership of our responsibilities, to be held accountable, and to receive the prayer of faith for healing. I say this; as it is imperative that you understand what repentance is, what it means to you, and how you benefit from it.

During my Christian experience, I have repented for various things hundreds of times. Some things I have asked for forgiveness of the same thing more than once, many times my repentance for a particular situation was for once only. Let me explain.

In my first marriage, there were forms of emotional abuse my children experienced within our household. Once God dealt with my own heart and way of thinking, I could see the problem and that it was not going to fix itself or merely go away. I began to think differently and implement different actions that I had not done before. I also went to each of my children, confessing what I had knowingly done or allowed to happen to them, expressed my own contorted view, and asked for their forgiveness. I had to take responsibility for the parts that I had played in the relationship. I had to get a new attitude and decide to do something different. I had to seek God and see how He thought about the matter and by faith receive His forgiveness. My children were gracious as most children are and they granted the reprieve.

Now that they are older, they understand things differently from when they were children, sometimes it hurts, therefore, anger, resentment, and mistrust spring forth. At times I have been faced with difficult conversations because sometimes one of the children still feel hurt. At this point, I am no longer repenting because I already think, act, and have a new behavior about the old problem we previously mentioned. Instead, in this case, I acknowledge their feelings, ask them to forgive me, and express my love toward them. When I unintentionally do something that offends or is not Christ represented in my thinking, attitude, and behavior toward them for any reason, I will repent to them for that thing.

Repentance happens after you realize you have strayed away from God's prescribed way of thinking and now you see your error, change your thoughts, and thus change your attitude and behavior to align itself with God's intellect, character, and practice.
If someone repents to you and continues to act the same way, they did not sincerely repent. They merely confessed they hurt you and never changed their intent not to harm you again. They only acknowledged what they did to you. To repent, one has to have a change of the mind. One has to think in a way that God comprehends.

In the book of Acts, we see the life of Saul turned to Paul. Saul was a devout Jew with Roman citizenship who persecuted the church with pride, for money. Saul believed he was doing the will of the Father and thus was a good Jew and an honorable citizen. Saul, an unbelieving sinner, did not recognize the construct of his heart. Saul soon became aware of his sin when he heard the audible voice of the Lord speak to him and ask why he was persecuting Christ. He was struck blind and led to the house of a follower of Christ to receive the truth, repent, and recover from his blindness.

Saul only became Paul because he changed the way he thought! This change in his thoughts caused him to change his attitude and behaviors. His heart and mind became wholly transformed by the renewing of his mind. He no longer wanted to kill

Christians; he wanted to be one of them. Repentance happens when we think like, act like, and live like Christ. It is not by our ability but by the goodness of God shown in the scriptures as such: "Or despisest thou the riches of his goodness and forbearance and longsuffering; not knowing that the goodness of God leadeth thee to repentance" (Romans 2:4).

To stop smoking, drinking, partying, cheating, lusting, or any other fruit of sin we can think of is not repenting. The act of repentance is to stop accepting the way you reason as if it is the only truth and instead agree with how God considers a matter. Next, change your attitude, and thus you are free to change your behavior. Your changed behavior is a by-product of repenting. If you try to change your behavior but do not change the way you think, by definition, you have not repented. You have changed your behavior and are subject to find yourself in that same behavior again.

However, if you allow the goodness of God to come to you and love you as He points out your toxic thinking, you can choose to be sorry for your actions, change your mind, and submit your attitude to Him. Then your behavior will willfully change on its own. It is the fruit of your repentance.

THINK LIKE GOD REMINDERS

"Do the riches of his extraordinary kindness make you take him for granted and despise him? Haven't you experienced how kind and understanding he has been to you? Don't mistake his tolerance for acceptance. Do you realize that all the wealth of his extravagant kindness is meant to melt your heart and lead you into repentance?   Romans 2:4 TPT

Understand that when you are in a bad, sinful, and ugly place God is still with you and He is leading you to repentance. As you experience His sweetness, grace, love, and compassion acknowledge Him. Ask Him to help you desire to think like He thinks.

List two personal scriptures that God has given you about *repentance*:

1) _____
_____
_____
_____
_____

2) _____
_____
_____
_____
_____

What three steps will you take to implement the above scriptures?

1) _____
2) _____
3) _____

Chapter 6
HOW IT WORKS

I would like to present to you a true story shared in the books of Exodus and Numbers vividly painting us a vicarious episode in the lives of the children of Israel. A people God chose to display His glory through. Due to their unwillingness to obey the commandments of their God, they found themselves like sheep led to the slaughter. They once experienced freedom, wealth, and vitality among their people before the dictates of slavery came to engulf them like a Sahara dust storm in Egypt. They were eventually taken captive in Egypt and were bound in the chains of their minds. For ten generations and four hundred years they were beaten, degraded, made to feel subhuman and killed. God had grand plans for them.

From the least likely place emerged a deliverer. Not just any rebel but one of their kin, as a matter of fact, before a firm decision finalized, he was a double-agent defending the rights of the people while hiding under royal palace robes. Only after committing murder did Moses feel defeated in his humanitarian efforts to protect right against wrong. He fled to Midian in desperation and self-preservation. There he settled, married, and found *his* deliverer!

After his burning bush experience and much convincing, Moses consents to God's way of thinking, he accepted his life was not in vain and the heartfelt desire to deliver his people was an acceptable desire. It only needed to be submitted to The Deliverer. Moses repented in his thoughts. He changed his thinking to align itself to the commandments or to God's prescribed way of thinking. Moses rejected being an unbeliever and a sinner as in the beginning, deciding not to argue with God about his speech, about how the people would not believe him, and about sending someone else. He instead conceded and accepted God's miracles.

After many miracles to prove to the people and Pharaoh that God had sent him, Moses became like a rock. He became unwavering. Moses was applying all that had been learned, to deliver his people, to himself first. He wanted them to learn how to begin to think another way, in doing so their actions would align with Gods prescribed way of thinking. Moses was repentant and became a believer. He then went forward and began to obey what he heard God say for him to do.

Getting hundreds of thousands, possibly millions of his kin to think as God thinks was no small task. Moses worked hard at it, and God was consistent. God had displayed His strong hand for the children of Israel by performing many miracles. One after the other He eventually annihilated their enemy at the Red Sea. The children of Israel used their first gift, the power of choice to be unbelieving, sinful, with hearts deafened to the commandments of God.

As the story continues to unfold, we find in the book of Numbers that Moses brings his followers to the edge of Canaan in the wilderness of Paran. Following the way God thinks, he sends out twelve spies, one man from each tribe, to survey the land and to report back to the rest of Israel. Their task was straight forward and specific.

They were to go northwest by way of Negev into the hill country. They were to see what the land was like if it would be suitable for farming and grazing, could it accommodate their needs, were the people of the land strong or weak, was the land protected by walls and were their borders? They were instructed to enter the territory and bring back proof of its substance since it was the season for the harvesting of grapes.

The twelve were stealth, shrewd, wise, and obedient. These men surveyed all the land as instructed not leading on to their true intentions. They journeyed and saw the inhabitants as well as the spoils. They even renamed the land Eshcol or "cluster" because of the bounty they found of figs, pomegranates, and grapes so large it took two men to carry one cluster on a pole between them. The land was just what they wanted. It was just what God had promised, it could accommodate all their needs, and there was room for the Israelites to flourish. The soil was prolific, and the water source was plenteous. It was good land. Just like God promised, a land flowing with milk and honey. They could not have been in a more prosperous territory if they had been in the nation of Egypt itself; because this place was prepared just for them.

Use your imagination if you can, the journey home was forty days away. During that time the men slept in the hills and rocks of the mountains. They recalled their stealth maneuvers and praised one another's cunning sight, tactics, and intuitiveness. They howled and hurled praises of their ability to interject themselves and then disappear without a trace. They rejoiced at their skill and looking at the bounty they gathered, reminded them all the more of their success.

There was one slight problem; however, an outsider was among them. An influence strong and invisible to the naked eye. He had been watching them the entire time. He had journeyed with them from Paran and watched the whole scene take place. On the way home, he watched as they cheered and danced the further away, they got from Canaan. He considered his opportune time, place, and person to express himself through. He found one, one of the twelve who without words kept envisioning the giants of Anak. The influencer brought nightmares and found one, then another who feared what they saw in their dreams.

He waited patiently, watching, influencing, and interjecting in their thoughts pictures and visions the way he wanted them to see it. Almost home, they were almost back to the wilderness; they were only a few days away when the Influencer decided this was his perfect opportunity. In their mind's eye, several men began to see the giants, how their enemies would take over the land, the war that would ensue, and how the giants of Anak would overtake them. They saw the battle in their mind. The giants would conquer four Israelites at a time, slashing the throats of their loved ones and devastating their women and children.

Finally, at the campfire when they were about twelve days out one of the men made the atmosphere solemn. "I had a dream last night. The scene was worse than Egypt. Our people were assailed by an army of Amalekites, Jebusites, Hittites, and coming up from behind them all, were the sons of Anak throwing spears. They overtook our strongest fighters and stripped our women of their innocence. We cannot attack them else they devastate us." An influence of fear waved throughout the camp, and it touched one, then another, then another. All twelve men heard and felt the sting of these thoughts and suggestions. Ten men agreed with what they heard and felt. Two men rejected what they heard and felt.

By the time they had made it home the men were no longer celebrating their successful and cunning maneuvers. Instead, they were bickering and arguing, fearful of what was next. When they arrived at the camp, Moses, Aaron, the other leaders and the children of Israel all awaited the spies report. One after another they told of the green land, plush trees, and bountiful water supply. They heard gasps erupt as they uncovered the enormous branches of grape clusters and the wheel barrel display of figs and pomegranates.

The people were excited then suddenly, like a well-timed incision it began all over again. "However," one of the spies began, "the land is so large it will engulf us!" "Yes" another one added, "and we will be defeated if we try to take it." A spy named Caleb interjected, "Wait, it is a good land, it will accommodate our children's children and us. We should go up now and secure our inheritance." Another spy Joshua agreed and exclaimed with fervor, "God is on our side, we can take the land he promised." Grippingly, ten of the others began to protest even more. "There are giants in the land, and we will all perish if we go up against them."

Satan, the influencer was ready! He had been hovering over them the entire time. Now, as a gentle breeze swaying over the heads of the people, this Influencer of fear methodically penetrated the whole camp. Imparting his images and ideas to join with their visions and ideas. The people began to complain and murmur against Moses and Aaron. They wished they could return to Egypt plotting to find a leader to take them back. They blamed God saying He only wanted to lead them to Canaan to die. They complained all day and cried out against their leaders all through the night. Longing to stone Caleb and Joshua. The Influencer was elated, and his poisonous tactic was spreading like wildfire. Even better, the people agreed with him. Their unbelief, sin, and obstinance were like fresh oxygen on a small flickering flame. His job here was complete and he was off to create havoc somewhere else.

The outcome was disastrous. God wanted to annihilate them, but Moses pleaded with God explaining that the other nations would say God could not deliver His people from the wilderness. So instead, by the laws of nature, just as it happened to their ancestors Adam and Eve they eventually died. It took forty years before those who agreed with their way of thinking and the Influencer of fear, to die off from among them. It took forty years before Caleb and Joshua would finally obtain the precious promise which they were so eager about in their youth. Within one generation; and Moses himself would not even enter into the beautiful land. Instead, he would be buried by God after his death.

Many times, we are no different from the children of Israel when we complain and pout about the way our life is going when we have obeyed what he has told us to do. We often envision that because we are obedient, our path will be flawless, there will be the smell of fresh cut flowers and bright lights to illuminate our way. In reality, God gives us a promise. He tells us how he thinks about a situation and then asks us to partner with Him. Sometimes we partner, and sometimes we refuse, but every time it begins with our thoughts.

God had revealed himself to the children of Israel through many miracles, He then appointed them a leader, and all the while He instructed them to rehearse and accept the promises that He gave them. "See, I am sending my angel before you to lead you safely to the land I have prepared for you" (Exodus 23:20 NLT). Before the Israelites ever reached the edge of Paran, God had promised to send an angel to go before them to ensure their safety and success. They only had to agree with the promise. You are the same, God has revealed Himself to you through His scripture and told you what He would do for you. You merely have to agree with his way of thinking.

As the Influencer of fear came to the Israelites, and they partnered with him instead of God, that generation lost their promise. They decided to live with a thought that nurtured and caressed their unbelief and sin.

When an influencer of doubt, disbelief, fear, or sin comes to you are you like the children of Israel? Do you complain and accuse

God of doing something wrong or leading you into a void space? May I suggest that you rewind your experience and see what part you played in the beginning. Were your thoughts a culprit in the descending spiral of misery. Did you agree with the influencer of fear and take a road that caused you to perish? Have you agreed with unforgiveness and are now living with pain and confusion in your body and mind? What do you do with thoughts that you hear that oppose the way God thinks? Do you agree with them and let them dictate to you what you will be and where you will go? Alternatively, do you grab the thought, cast it down to the ground, stomping on it, and then accept God's way of thinking?

Graciously, we have a perfect covenant through Jesus Christ. For with the presentation of Christ, we also received His Holy Spirit. His Spirit leads and guides us to hear the truth or accept God's prescribed way of thinking as the scripture states. "However when He, the Spirit of Truth, is come, He will guide you into all truth; for He shall not speak from Himself, but whatsoever He shall hear, that shall He speak; and He will show you things to come" (John 16:13KJV). If you have never asked Jesus the Son of God to come into your heart and to become Lord (or owner) of your life, then you will not be able to participate in the beautiful transformation that you read here.

Fear not! God has made provision even for you. Yes, this book is one listed on your path(s). The two of you talked about this place before time began and He said, "Here I will give you an opportunity to receive of my Spirit!" The choice you make will determine what direction you will head down next. May I implore you to choose Jesus now! It is as simple as a prayer request to God in the name of His Son Jesus. The scripture tells us that 'if we confess with our mouth the Lord Jesus and believe in our heart that God raised him from the dead then we will be saved' (Romans 10:9-10). If you want the benefits of thinking like God but have never accepted him, pray this with me and He will receive you into the kingdom of God with all rights, privileges, and authority that comes with it.

"Father, I confess with my mouth that Jesus is the Son of God, whom you raised from the dead and who is now my blood brother. I welcome Jesus into my heart, and I receive the Holy Spirit who is there to help me learn, grow, and understand the mind of God. I change the way I have been thinking. I reject being an unbeliever. Instead, I agree with your prescribed way of thinking. Your Holy Bible is true, and I agree with everything in it. It is your thoughts about the best way for me and what will make me prosperous. Thank you for restoring me to my rightful place in the kingdom, in Jesus name Amen."

Now if you prayed that prayer in your heart and believed it, Jesus has now filled your Spirit with himself. I encourage you to contact our office and let us know of the great news and please connect with your local church that is teaching the word of God. Making a connection to your local church will give you strength and support as you grow. Read your bible; which is the blueprint of how God thinks, and it shows you how to reason like God. Welcome to the family! We rejoice with you like all of the angels in heaven rejoice, Luke 15:10 (Nelson, 1990). If you do not have a bible, contact our office, and we will provide you with one.

Now that you have received Christ into your heart or if you otherwise remember who He is to you, I want to leave you with this final thought. Psalm 139:13-18 in the Passion Translation helps us experience the beauty and purpose that the Creator has for each humankind.

"You formed my innermost being, shaping my inside and my intricate outside, and wove them all together in my mother's womb. I thank you, God, for making me so mysterious! Everything you do is marvelously breathtaking. It amazes me to think about it! How thoroughly you know me, Lord! You even formed every bone in my body when you created me in the secret place, carefully, skillfully, shaping me from nothing to something. You saw who you created me to be before I became me! Written in your book, before I'd ever seen the light of day, are the number of days you planned for me. Every single moment you are thinking of me! How precious and beautiful to consider that you cherish me perpetually in your every thought! Oh God, your desires toward me are more than the grains of sand on the shore! When I awake each morning, you are still with me."

God perpetually thinks of you! He has purposed you! God has made you! He loves you! Never forget!

"Here is my conclusion: Fear God and obey his commands, for this is the duty of every person" (Ecclesiastes 12:13 NLT). This author has the same conclusion as the author of Ecclesiastes. Reverence, respect, honor, acknowledge, obey, and adhere to God's prescribed way of thinking to obtain a fulfilled purpose.

DEFINITIONS

KNEW - is described as to ascertain by seeing, to observe, to care, to recognize, acknowledge, acquaintance, advise, answer, comprehend, cunning, diligent, discern, discover, endued with, familiar friend, perceive, prognosticate, regard, have respect, to teach and to understand. Pg. 20

"This is an exchange between you and God. He does the above things to you and you do those to Him. It denotes the consistent movement of an ebb and flow relationship."

COMMANDMENT- translates to God's prescribed way of thinking. In many cases, the word commandment is interchangeable with "word" and the "law" in both the old and new testament.

Pg. 32

SIN – joining your will to think in a way that opposes the way God thinks which leads to actions that oppose the desires, purposes, nature, and plans of God. Pg. 46

UNBELIEF – is to stubbornly refuse to believe and act in agreement with Gods prescribed way of thinking, His desires, purposes, and plans.

Pg. 55

REPENT - means to change your thoughts, attitudes, and behaviors to align with God's prescribed way of thinking.

Pg. 66

BOOK REVIEWS FROM YOU!

Dear reader, we at Kingdom Thinking Enterprises pray that this book has made an impact in your life. If you agree, please find us on Instagram or YouTube and share a sixty second book review or a comment. May your life and your prescribed way of thinking be forever changed!

YouTube WRITTEN COMMENTS:

YouTube: Kingdom Thinking Enterprises

Go to the Think Like God video and post your reviews

UPLOAD Instagram VIDEOS BELOW:

@denitrabrownnme
@kingdomthinkingenterprises

www.ingramcontent.com/pod-product-compliance
Lightning Source LLC
Chambersburg PA
CBHW052112070526
44584CB00017B/2456